Giselle Dundas
Lose 5lbs in 5 Days!
IBO 34374922
www.sipteawithg.com

Before — After
(407) 900-4506

Actual Results

TLC IBO
TOTAL LIFE CHANGES
INDEPENDENT BUSINESS OWNER

JAFRA BEAUTY TIP

Marilyn King
JAFRA Independent Consultant

443-803-2999

shellk423@gmail.com
www.myjafra.com/marilynking

Be All You Can Be!

Experience wonderful products and learn how to earn income.

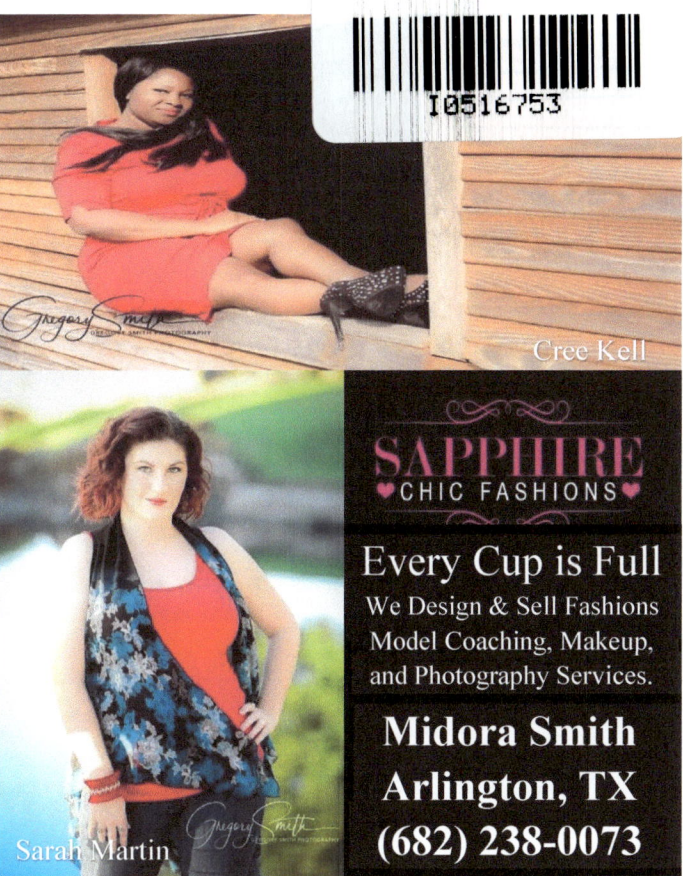

Cree Kell

SAPPHIRE CHIC FASHIONS

Every Cup is Full
We Design & Sell Fashions
Model Coaching, Makeup,
and Photography Services.

Midora Smith
Arlington, TX
(682) 238-0073

Sarah Martin

WARRENDA KING
Fashion Stylist & Owner of
GeeChee Gal Vintage Boutique
4273 Washington Rd
Atlanta, GA 30344

We Love to Provide Our Customers with One of A Kind Statement Pieces.

Atlanta Top Stylists Pull From Our Racks!

FB/IG : geecheegalvintage

Meet Sheila- The Credit Boss

Bad Credit? I Can Help!

(510) 736-2402

@sheilathecredit_boss

www.fseconnect.net/SPullum

ATIYA MCNEAL
INDEPENDENT BEAUTY CONSULTANT
(336) 831-7700

"From innovative skin care to on-trend cosmetics and fragrances, Mary Kay offers products women and men love!"

ATIYAMCNEAL@MARYKAY.COM

WWW.MARYKAY.COM/ATIYAMCNEAL

Let me help you find your new favorites! Contact me to discover more.

Reading is FUNDAMENTAL

Reading is FUNDAMENTAL

Reading is FUNDAMENTAL

WWW.BLACKLYFEPUBLICATIONS.COM

Mnyama Nkosi and Jannah Malkia are the owners of Black Lyfe Company and Publications. They have given opportunities to inspiring author's to become actual authors! They are dedicated to their craft and the longevity of their authors. Black Lyfe Company and Publications is the voice for our people. Nkosi and Malkia take the literary world serious because it is a hard road. The knowledge that they both have as publishers and authors is taught daily.

Reading is FUNDAMENTAL

Reading is FUNDAMENTAL

Reading is FUNDAMENTAL

Norma's Bath & Body

Welcome to the Body Bakery! Norma's Bath & Body was established in 2004! Products are perfect for anyone! For women, kids, teens, men, and also a perfect gift for co-workers, nurses, teachers, family as well as yourself! The products are fruity with a variety of delicious scents. Products are available from goats milk glycerin soaps to gift baskets! The lotions are made with Shea Butters, they soften the skin nicely!

Follow Us on FB: Norma's Bath and Body
We Accept Wholesale Orders!

Email normasbathandbody@gmail.com
www.normasbathandbody.artfire.com

DIVA COSMETICZ
Where fierce meets fashionista

Diva Cosmeticz are all natural handmade cosmetics, made with vegan mica and natural oils, such as grapeseed, coconut oils, shea butter, and vitamin E. Diva Cosmeticz has been around for four years. Our products can be found at the website below.

WWW.ETSY.COM/DIVACOSMETICZ

 @DIVACOSMETICZ

VIRTUAL COOKING CLASSES
W/ CHEF KAMI REDD

I WILL GUIDE YOU THROUGH 3 BASIC HEALTHY RECIPES/SEASONING BLEND & EVEN HAVE YOU MAKING YOUR FAVORITE MEALS. EACH SESSION IS 1.5 HOURS

$45 PER SESSION

WWW.CHEFKAMIREDD.ONLINE

SEA SALT & AVOCADO
Pink sea salt, Valencia orange and creamy avocado

HTTPS://CINDYROMAN.SCENTSY.US/
Warmers | lotions | bath bombs & more!

Sweet Surrender is a small home-based business in Henderson, NV that is focused on providing high quality, organic, luxury skin care products that are safe, gentle, and nourishing for use from the youngest to the most mature member of the household.

All products are handmade in small batches so attention to detail, care, and quality are never sacrificed.

Joy Edwards
Owner & Mastercrafter

My Beautiful Fluff

Welcome to My Beautiful Fluff. The shop that makes women stand up and be proud of their curves.

APPAREL — T-SHIRTS — CLOTHING

EARRINGS — CANVAS BAGS — ACCESSORIES

Contact Brittany Washington
(563) 447-0836
www.mybeautifulfluff.com
info@mybeautifulfluff.com

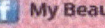 My Beautiful Fluff   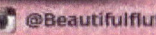 @Beautifulfluff

Sweet Surrender Handmade Bath & Body Essentials

www.sweet-surrender.biz

Sensationally Nappy

One evening, back in 2014, Lori Scott decided she was tired of perms, scarves, or laying on her face to keep her hair from being ruined, in other words trying to keep it in place. No matter what the cut or style was, she was simply unhappy with her hair. After debating, she decided to do the BIG CHOP! This was one of the best decisions in her life! Lori loves everything about the *Natural Hair Movement*, from the twist outs, braid outs, bandu knots and more! Locally, she could not find any t-shirts that celebrated natural hair and that is how **Sensationally Nappy** was born.

It's not just hair. It's a movement!

WWW.SENSATIONALLYNAPPY.COM

FOLLOW US ON TWITTER, FB, GOOGLE+, IG

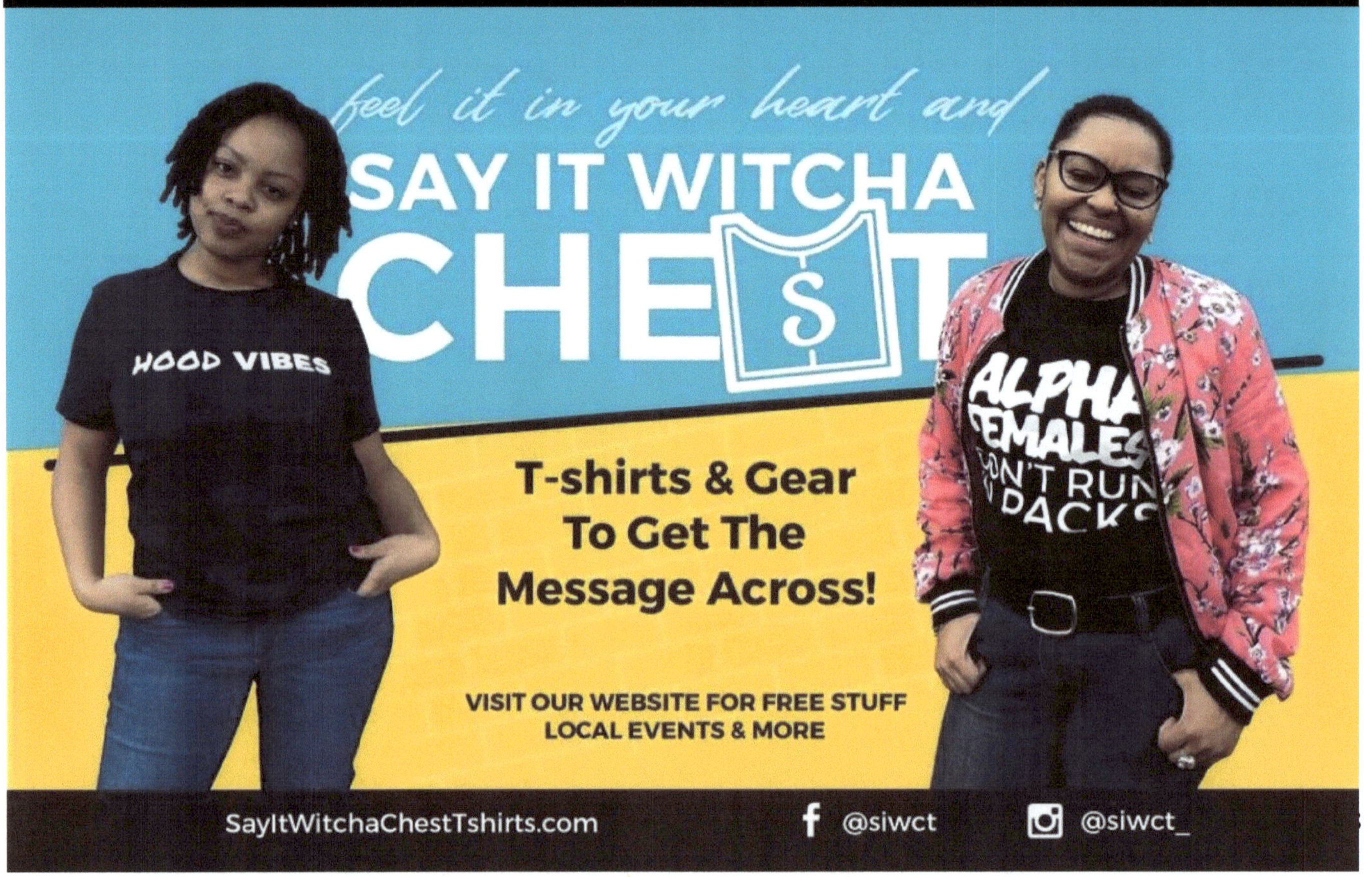

---

feel it in your heart and
SAY IT WITCHA CHEST

T-shirts & Gear To Get The Message Across!

VISIT OUR WEBSITE FOR FREE STUFF
LOCAL EVENTS & MORE

SayItWitchaChestTshirts.com   @siwct   @siwct_

We help small businesses enhance brand awareness, improve client acquisition, and increase employee retention with customized promotional products and services.

Are You Ready To Stand Out?

WWW.MIXXEDMARKETING.COM

Here at Glamorous Trois Hair Extensions, we recognize the temple of every woman and our beauty is tied into our hair. I started Glamorous Trois Hair Extensions. Giving every woman the confidence and ability to feel and look beautiful. Glamorous Trois Hair is 100% unprocessed, grade AAA human hair.

"A Glamorous Look for a Glamourous You"

3Js Creation Production Company

www.eventwire.com/b/3jscreation-production-company-staten-island-ny/7a94dc5ea79beb7f

We desire to create all that you can imagine while keeping you within an economical budget. Our Services include but are not limited to: Complete Event Setup & Breakdown, Centerpieces, Favors, Balloon Arch Columns, Variety of Linen (chairs and tables) and much more!
We pride our business on serving its community and providing clientele with the most memorable event EVER.

3JsCreation serves as a multi-event planning and production service to its community. Owner, Shaquana Perry Garcia, a Staten Island native, designed 3Js Creation for the "working family on a budget." Her creative DIY projects and special event gatherings were a community phenomenon! Mrs. Garcia's mission was to secure her families' financials all while expanding her visual arts and creative network.

SAMPLE MEAL PREP MENU

BREAKFAST
Gluten Free Peanut Butter Waffles w/Strawberries & Raw Honey
(615 calories)

SNACK 1
Quaker Popped Rice Crisp
(130 calories)

LUNCH
Baked Buffalo Chicken Casserole w/Spinach Salad
(582 calories)

SNACK 2
Pineapple w/Low-Fat Cottage Cheese
(151 calories)

DINNER
Turkey Burger w/Mushroom Bun & Sweet Potato Fries
(399 calories)

SNACK 3
Blueberry Protein Pops
(76.25 calories)

"Let me cook you to a healthier lifestyle"

CHEF KAMI'S MEAL PLANNING & PREP

PROFESSIONAL CHEF
CERTIFIED MEDICAL NUTRITIONIST

WEEKLY SERVICE
21 Snacks & Meals for $180

CALL 240-670-KAMI(5264)
WWW.CHEFKAMIREDD.ONLINE

The Power Of Hygiene

Cherish™ is a sanitary napkin that provides you with the dryness, comfort and protection that you need and want, without the health risks. It helps protect against germs and bacteria, helps to reduce inflammation, fights against vaginal irritations and infections and reduces unwanted odor.

Meredith Franklin

Distributor ID: 11790130
Email: healthywithmeredith@gmail.com
Instagram: @mmfranklin4
Ready to order?
healthywithmeredith.myitworks.com
Online catalog:
https://static.myitworks.com/partypad/en-us/

Poetry Corner

Mark Edwards

"...follow your heart and write with your soul..."

Mark believes having love for old school rap music and the stories told, secretly embedded with him. Not limiting the special shout outs mentioned such as Grand Master Flash and the Furious Five who rapped songs like, *The Message* and *White Lines*, Slick Rick who rapped *Children's Story* and *Mona Lisa*. Even Nas with his phenomenal collaboration with Lauryn Hill *If I Ruled the World*, alongside so many other rappers who vividly relayed a story inspired him to be the poet he is today.

Mark's poetry style is closest to "Imagery Poetry". He writes in a way where the reader will come one with his words, visually see the message, and feel the images of the poetry he places before you. He writes more sensual poetry on love and romance, and truly tries to have the reader become one with his mind as if they are either in the story or have lived or even desired to recreate what is being written.

When it comes to having a personal favorite poet, Mark doesn't necessarily have one. He has read the works of James Weldon Johnson, Maya Angelou, and Langston Hughes to name a few. He then mentioned that he tries not to read other people's poetry in fear that he will become trapped into their style of writing and thinking. Although, he is a true believer in supporting the works of other writers, meaning he will buy others' books to support. Mark isn't a stranger to the meaning of support either; in his second book, *Morning Coffee*, he had a young woman by the name of Sharon Rhodes add two of her pennings to the book. As well as his third book, *Afternoon Devotion: Two Hearts One Soul*, he had the honor of allowing two other poets, Sheila Taylor and A. Melody Kaye add their phenomenal poetic responses to his writings.

His advice to other aspiring poets is to follow your heart and write with your soul. Whereas he writes more to love, romance and sensuality, other poets may feel deeper on issues from politics, to life's hardships, to the mental and physical religion. So, no matter what the topic is- follow your heart, write from the inner soul of you, and remember you will never be able to please everyone who reads your poetry but the few who you do touch and connect with are worth a million nonbelievers.

Available at
lulu.com/spotlight/MEdwards

Bad Kompany Incorporated

CEO | Founder | Author
Rodney Dewayne

Rodney Dewayne published his first book self-titled *The Best Poet You Know*, which instantly was a huge success, also earning himself a five star review. Satisfying his fans and readers throughout the country. The book is available on Amazon, Barnes & Nobles, and Kindle and from the artist himself when he is on road trips sharing his gift wherever there is a microphone and a listener.

The best poet you know

Contact information

(817) 435-0646

 @Rodneyyyw

 @RodneyDewayne

SASHA TAYLOR
www.Primerica.com/SashaTaylor
Senior Representative
(610) 718-6473

P R I M E R I C A

Become Financially Free!
Making Money
Saving Money

Primerica is a Main Street company for Main Street North America. My mission is to help families earn more income and become properly protected, debt free and financially independent.

YOUR DONATIONS WILL PROVIDE VETERANS WITH THE MEANS TO ACHIVE A BETTER LIFE.

Greatness Pursued
PLEASE DONATE ON:
www.GreatnessPursued.org

Drink 2 cups of tea a day... lose 5 lbs in 5 days!

www.TransformDaNewYou.com
Shakeerah Houchens
443.255.8534

Lose 5lbs in 5days!

Pleasure Talk with Amber
Dare to Go There
Tune in to Pleasure Talk w/ Amber where no topic is taboo.
www.pleasuretalkwithamber.com

PLATINUM PLEASURES
For all of your erotic endeavors

- Adult Novelties
- Educational Services
- Platinum Pleasure Parties

Amber Jones
616.329.8654
amberjones@platinumpleasures.net

www.platinumpleasures.net

Platinum Pleasures

Travel agent
I'm here to make your vacation dreams come true.
Ashley Weeams
870-898-0685
Facebook & Instagram
Thetravelingdiva17
Website - https://evotravelagent.com/thetravelingdiva

Travel Time

Natural Bodycare

Sister Sankofa Natural Bodycare

- Whipped Shea Butter
- Face/Body Scrubs
- Bath Bombs
- Handmade Soap
- Lip Balm
- Hair Creams, and more!

Save 10% off your next order with code: "ELITE10"

www.SisterSankofaNaturalBodycare.com

Offer Valid until 12/31/2018

Running Your Race, LLC

CEO/Founder – Dr. April J. Lisbon

Services Offered – Family Coaching & Empowerment Speaking

Contact Information:

advocacycoaching@gmail.com

(540) 300-7928

in www.linkedin.com/in/aprillisbonpeoples/

f www.facebook.com/theadvocacycoach

t https://twitter.com/raiseurvisions

Consult Positivity, LLC

Samantha R. White, C.P.C.

Samantha empowers women of color to tackle their thoughts, emotions, and finances through virtual coaching sessions and financial packages!

www.consultpositivity.com

Email: findpeace@consultpositivity.com

(910) 370-8986

"Change your mindset, change your life!"

Althea Webber-Bates
Project Resiliency

Project Resiliency started with a vision by Althea Webber Bates to support women in embracing the fact that they don't always have to be strong. We, as women of color can uplift each other because supporting my sister in her time of need provides healing and resiliency to both of us.

Mission

Project Resiliency is social movement that seeks to encourage and empower women of color in areas of self-care and resiliency related to mental, physical and emotional health while providing connectivity and supports to other women of color through resiliency circles, conferences, workshops and seminars.

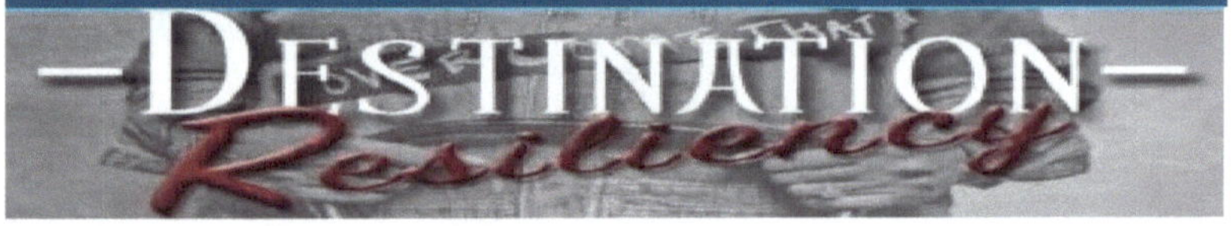

DESTINATION Resiliency

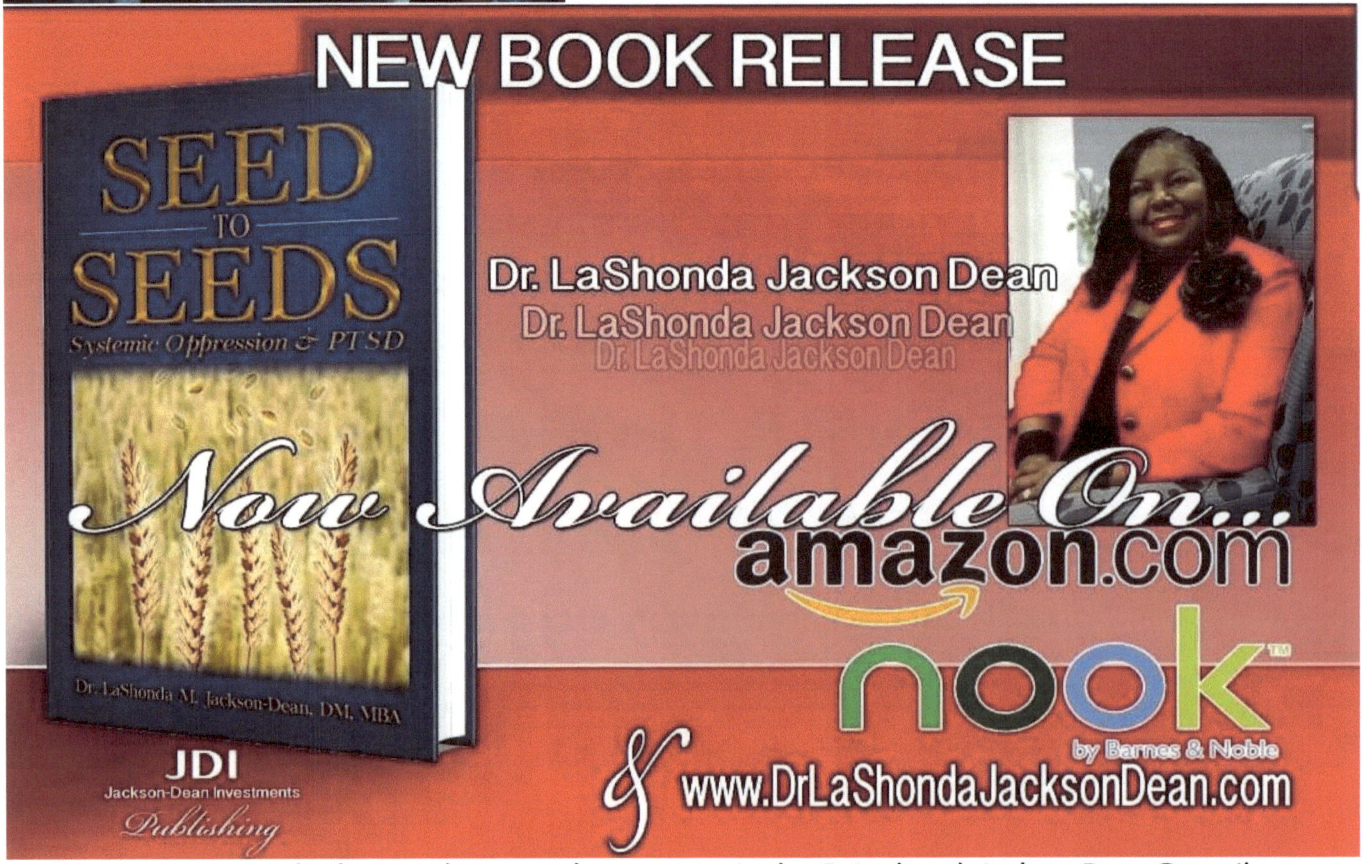

NEW BOOK RELEASE

SEED TO SEEDS
Systemic Oppression & PTSD

Dr. LaShonda M. Jackson-Dean, DM, MBA

JDI
Jackson-Dean Investments
Publishing

Dr. LaShonda Jackson Dean

Now Available On...
amazon.com
nook™ by Barnes & Noble
www.DrLaShondaJacksonDean.com

For an unautographed copy, please send request to AuthorDrLashondaJacksonDean@gmail.com

The Beauty of Credit

Danielle Gaspard, MBA
Credit Repair Specialist
(914) 640-0348
www.beautyofcredit.com

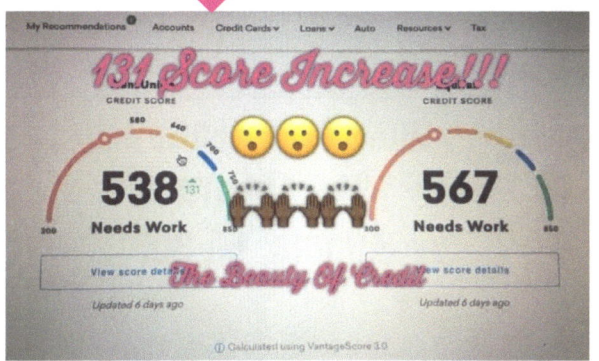

Love's Therapeutics

Love's Therapeutics was birthed out of the need for quality skin care products suitable for all skin types. It became a mission to find suitable steroid free solution that could still be affective at healing the skin. This was the birth of Love's Therapeutics.

Experience Love's Therapeutics

@lovestherapeutics

@lovestherapeutics

www.lovestherapeutics.com

Featured Carriers

GeeChee Gal Vintage Boutique
4273 Washington Rd
Atlanta, GA 30344

Something Special Styling Salon
3317 Finley Rd. Suite #230
Irving, TX 75062

The Barber Lounge for Men
11850 Park Waldorf Ln. Ste 107
Waldorf, MD 20601

A Touch of Class Beauty Salon
1300 W Waco Dr
Waco, TX 76701

Quite Cocky Enterprises
396 Auburn Ave
Atlanta, GA 30312

TESTIMONIALS

"Thanks for what you are Doing to promote and market small businesses."
-The Barber Lounge for Men

"Yes! Glad I got a copy. Clients enjoyed it over the past few days!"
-Miss Jazz Salon

"This will be the best decision that you'll ever make for your business."
-Norma Groves McElroy

"Truly appreciate you and your publication…"
-Author Mark Edwards

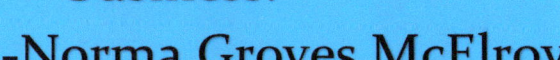

HAVE FEEDBACK?
SEND IT OUR WAY!

NEED ADVERTISEMENT?

www.DiamondEliteMagazine.com

Diamond Elite Magazine is a quarterly magazine with surprise special edition issues. The goal of this journey is to boost the exposure of small business by sending this magazine to independent carriers across the United States.

 @DIAMONDELITEMAGAZINE

 @DIAMONDELITEMAGAZINE

www.ingramcontent.com/pod-product-compliance
Lightning Source LLC
Chambersburg PA
CBHW051836210526
45473CB00005B/1896